FEB 0 3 2015

W9-BSD-344

Patterns in the DESERT

by Joyce Markovics

Consultant: Kimberly Brenneman, PhD
National Institute for Early Education Research, Rutgers University
New Brunswick, New Jersey

BEARPORT
PUBLISHING

New York, New York

Credits

Cover, © Yvette Cardozo/Alamy; 3, © carterito/Thinkstock; 4–5, © Lenar Musin/Shutterstock; 6, © Val Lawless/Shutterstock; 7, © Zvonimir Atletic/Shutterstock; 8–9, © Gary Nafis; 10–11, © Francois Gohier; 12–13, © Franz Aberham/Getty Images; 14–15, © Yvette Cardozo/Alamy; 16–17, © Jane Sweeney/Getty Images; 18–19, © Tony Camacho/ScienceSource; 20–21, © Susan E. Degginger/Alamy; 22–23, © Matt Jeppson/Shutterstock; 24–25, © orxy/Shutterstock; 26–27, © Gerold & Cynthia Merker/Visuals Unlimited, Inc.; 28–29, © Gilad Malenky/Alamy; 30A, © jmb/Shutterstock; 30B, © Pakhnyushcha/Shutterstock; 30C, © Arnoud Quanjer/Shutterstock; 30D, © NHPA/SuperStock; 31TL, © Gary Nafis; 31TR, © Tony Camacho/ScienceSource; 31BL, © orxy/Shutterstock; 31BR, © Jane Sweeney/Getty Images.

Publisher: Kenn Goin
Senior Editor: Joyce Tavolacci
Creative Director: Spencer Brinker
Design: Debrah Kaiser
Photo Researcher: Michael Win

Library of Congress Cataloging-in-Publication Data

Markovics, Joyce L., author.
   Patterns in the desert / by Joyce Markovics.
      pages cm. — (Seeing patterns all around)
   Includes bibliographical references and index.
   ISBN-13: 978-1-62724-337-7 (library binding)
   ISBN-10: 1-62724-337-2 (library binding)
   1. Pattern perception—Juvenile literature. 2. Shapes—Juvenile literature. 3. Deserts—Juvenile literature. I. Title.
   BF294.M37 2015
   516.15—dc23
                              2014009071

For more information, write to Bearport Publishing Company, Inc., 45 West 21st Street, Suite 3B, New York, New York 10010. Printed in the United States of America.

10 9 8 7 6 5 4 3 2 1

Contents

Finding Patterns in the Desert

Patterns can be shapes, colors, or sizes that repeat over and over.

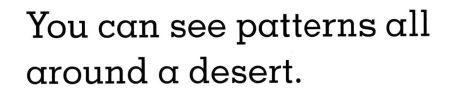

You can see patterns all around a desert.

Fur on camels can form a pattern.

Light, dark.

One round desert cactus is not a pattern.

It does not repeat.

Clumps of cactuses, however, form a pattern.

They make a pattern of spiky, round shapes.

Stripes on a lizard's back make a pattern.

Dark brown, yellow.

The colors repeat.

They make an **alternating** pattern.

9

A ringtail cat also has an alternating pattern on its body.

Its tail has black-and-white stripes.

The colored
stripes repeat.

Four meerkats form a pattern.

They look in different directions.

Right, left.

The pattern repeats.

13

A snake moves across the desert.

Its body makes a shape in the sand.

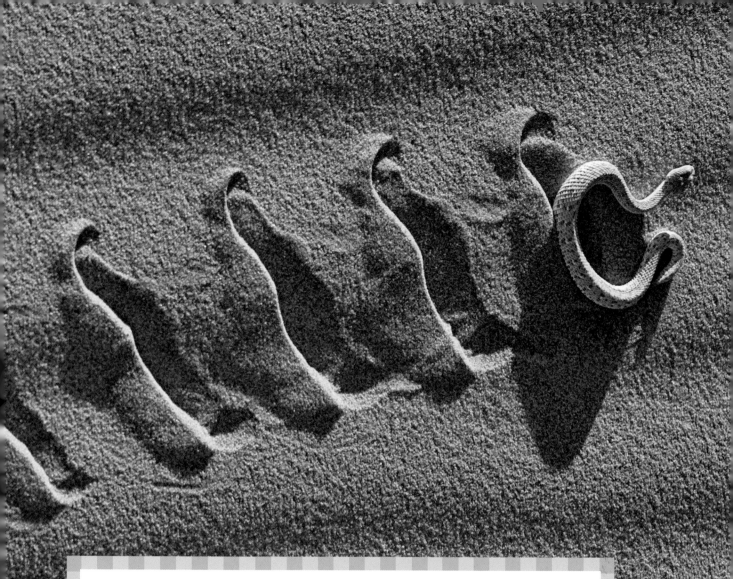

The shape repeats over
and over to form a pattern.

This building in the desert goes round and round.

It makes a **spiral** pattern.

17

A spotted hyena walks across the dry ground.

The spots on its coat are different sizes and shapes.

They make an **irregular pattern**.

Patterns can be colorful—and very beautiful.

Pink and yellow repeat on the petals of these cactus flowers.

21

The stripes on a snake's body also form a pattern of colors.

Black, white, black, red.

The pattern repeats over and over.

Patterns can cover a large area.

Wind makes **ripples** in the desert sand.

The pattern goes on and on.

25

Patterns can also be very small.

Each section of this centipede's body has two stripes and two legs.

This pattern repeats.

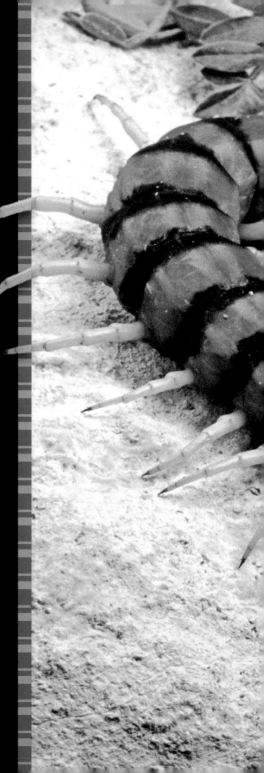

27

These palm trees make a pattern, too.

What pattern do you see?

Patterns are everywhere in a desert.

29

Explore More:
Which Pattern?

Look at the pictures. Each one shows a kind of pattern that can be found in the desert. Match each pattern with the correct picture.

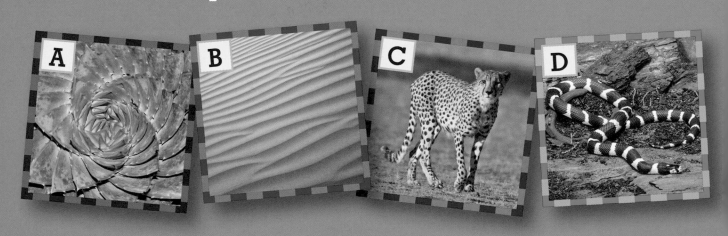

A

B

C

D

1. alternating pattern

2. wavy pattern

3. spiral pattern

4. irregular pattern

Answers are on page 32.

Glossary

alternating (AWL-tur-*nayt*-ing) changing back and forth, such as between two colors

irregular pattern (ih-REG-yuh-lur PAT-uhrn) a pattern that has one or more similar parts unequal in size, shape, or in the way they are arranged

ripples (RIP-uhls) small waves

spiral (SPYE-ruhl) winding or circling around a center

Index

Read More

Cleary, Brian P. *A–B–A–B–A: A Book of Pattern Play.* Minneapolis, MN: Millbrook Press (2010).

Pluckrose, Henry. *Pattern (Math Counts).* Chicago: Children's Press (1995).

Learn More Online

To learn more about patterns in the desert, visit
www.bearportpublishing.com/SeeingPatternsAllAround

About the Author

Joyce Markovics and her husband, Adam, live along the Hudson River in Tarrytown, New York.

Answers for Page 30:

1. D; 2. B; 3. A; 4. C